C000162163

Living
F R E E

A practical guide to mentoring and helping others
to live free from the web of internet pornography.

LIVING FREE

Copyright © 2008

Published by CARE

ISBN: 978-0-905195-06-3

British Library Cataloguing-in-Publication Data
A catalogue record for this book is available from the British Library

Cover and layout design by Going Public Design
Printed in 2008 in Great Britain

CARE is a well-established mainstream Christian charity providing resources and helping to bring Christian insight and experience to matters of public policy and practical caring initiatives. CARE is represented in the UK Parliaments and Assemblies, at the EU in Brussels and the UN in Geneva and New York.

CARE (Christian Action, Research & Education), a company limited by guarantee registered in England and Wales at 53 Romney Street, London, SW1P 3RF. Company No: 3481417, Charity No: 1066963, Scottish Charity No: SC038911

CARE:
Tel: 020 7233 0455
Email: mail@care.org.uk

www.care.org.uk

Contents

Acknowledgements

This handbook has been produced by CARE with contributions from Simon Bass, Chris Cordner, Dot Croall, Margaret Ellis, Rob Hodges, Richard Leahy-Jones, David Partington, Nola Leach and Claire Wilson-Thomas.

We are grateful to The Mandate for their help in making the publication of this book possible.

Introduction

In October 2004, I was privileged to chair 'Searching for Intimacy', a day conference hosted by CARE. The aim was to resource those involved in counselling and pastoral care on the topic of pornography addiction, particularly on the internet. This came about as a result of a previous survey of church leaders which revealed that pornography was a 'serious problem' within the Church. Almost all of the hundreds who replied – 86% – said they had not found any resources to assist them to support the men who had come to them for help.

CARE subsequently published the talks given at the conference in a book, *Searching for Intimacy*, and established a special website – www.care.org.uk/anon – which continues to provide practical advice for those struggling with internet pornography.

The purpose of this handbook is to give further practical help both to people who are caught in the web themselves and anyone who knows a person who is. It is written from a Christian viewpoint and presents accessible, concise information and encouragement to individuals, their wives and those who receive and offer pastoral and practical help. It also provides information for parents who want to protect their children from exposure to pornography.

Although most people who struggle with pornography are men, increasing numbers of women are using it too, whether in the company of a sexual partner or on their own. For convenience, this book usually uses 'he' and 'him' but we recognise that in some cases it will be 'she' and 'her'.

It is my heartfelt prayer that this handbook will encourage and equip and help all who seek to 'live free'.

Lyndon Bowring
Executive Chairman, CARE

Chapter 1
Understanding the Web

> *The moment sex ceases to be a servant it becomes a tyrant.*

G K Chesterton

Anyone who has struggled with pornography has met GK Chesterton's 'tyrant' and know from painful experience that it moves in, takes over and is never satisfied. As with all addictions, the very thing that seemed attractive, satisfying and fulfilling goes on to become an insatiable monster, demanding more and more time, energy, resources, self-esteem and confidence.

The nature of pornography

Pornography is intended to stimulate erotic thoughts. It uses the strong visual senses of men to promote lust, but promises the unreal, promoting false expectations of relationships. It is attractive to many. This should not surprise us: pornography is taking something inherently good – the sexual relationship between men and women, and twisting it. Overeating is a similar phenomenon: a short term enjoyable pastime of something that is meant to be beneficial to the human body, but in the long term, over-eating is destructive to an individual's health.

As human beings we all have a natural desire for closeness, intimacy, understanding, physical contact and comfort. Being sexually attracted to a person is normal and natural. But pornography gives false messages because it:

- shows women as mere physical objects and does not even try to show other ways in which a woman can be attractive, eg character, intelligence, humour
- shows sex as the only important thing in a relationship between a man and a woman
- cannot substitute for long-term love and commitment. It produces short-lived thrills and does nothing to develop a loving sexual relationship

In contrast, relationships motivated by love focus on the welfare of the other person and aim to be faithful to that person.

The draw of internet pornography seems to be greater than for any other type of media and it is widely accessible. More people are getting hooked. The difference is that internet pornography is **easily accessible, affordable and anonymous, and can appear secret and safe**. It is **interactive** in a way that is different to other media – new images are always available for the choosing, and there can be live interaction between real people in real time.

In the past, adults would have had to go looking specifically for pornography. Children were unlikely to have come across it, but now such material can be found accidentally on the internet whilst looking for innocent material. Over the last few years, the accessibility of the internet has mushroomed, giving great opportunities but also risks. It is not just through computers that adults and young people may be able to easily and secretly obtain large quantities of any sort of pornography, or sexually interact with others, but also through mobile phones and hand-held devices.

Losing out

It is not surprising that with so much material so easily accessible, some become trapped within their secret world of social and sexual fantasy, increasingly fearful of being found out – which further compounds feelings of loneliness and worthlessness. 'If they knew what I was really like they'd never want me.' 'If I tell them what goes on in my head they'll never talk to me again.'

John was avoiding applying for jobs; his friends saw him as lazy and often tried to challenge and motivate him into the workforce. As he explored these hesitations about work with a counsellor, it emerged that it stemmed from his fear that a few minutes of internet pornography use several years earlier would somehow come to light and be used against him. John was able to regain his confidence to venture out into the big wide world of work again when he realised that this was unlikely to come to light, nor was he the only job applicant likely to have used internet pornography.

This individual had only dabbled in the shallows of internet pornography, but even that had a debilitating effect on him. Research indicates that men are generally more likely to use pornography as a form of sexual fantasy than women, who tend to indulge in romantic escapism. This can become equally addictive and may lead on to them seeking out on-line relationships with real people. Some women become drawn into pornography by a sexual partner. One woman related how horrified she was to find herself accessing her husband's pornography while he was away. His use of pornography had been causing her great concern within their marriage and now it was becoming a personal issue for her as well. Individuals struggling with pornography and those close to them often live under a burden of shame and guilt which can persist and hold them back all their lives.

Attitudes to Pornography

There are a number of attitudes we can have towards pornography:

1. Considering it acceptable so we hardly think about it, unless it becomes an issue in the life of someone we care about.

2. Regarding pornography as dangerous and degrading, and therefore keeping clear and disapproving of anyone who acknowledges any connection with it.

3. Realising that this is more common than we would want to admit; that those caught up in pornography need help and acceptance and strong boundaries in their lives to bring them out of their addiction.

Our hope is that church leaders and friends will respond with compassionate understanding and grace towards people struggling with internet pornography. It would be tragic if those wanting to become free were put off seeking help because they feared being stigmatised with rejection and disapproval.

The nature of addiction and where it leads

Those using pornography can fall into three main categories:

1. Becoming interested in pornography, regularly accessing it on a computer, thinking it is not really harmful.

2. Being attracted to pornography even though they know it is wrong. Even though they try to stop accessing it they frequently give in to temptation.

3. Becoming attracted by pornography and gradually hooked until they realise it has turned into a tyrant ruling and ruining their lives and relationships.

The evidence certainly points to pornography being addictive for *some* people. Pornography stimulates the pleasure centre in the brain. But after a while, more pornography is needed to produce the same effect. The addictive cycle is started. Then there is an increase in intensity in the addiction so that the individual needs stronger material to get the same affect, moving on to the accepting of behaviour that previously they would have found unacceptable, and then the ultimate acting out of images seen in pornography.

A personal checklist

Answering the questions below can indicate whether you (or someone you know) have an addiction to internet pornography:

1. Do you regularly spend time looking for sexual stimulation on the internet (pornography, sexual/romantic chat rooms, etc)?

2. Have you tried to stop your involvement with internet pornography, but been unable?

3. Does your involvement with internet sex interfere with your physical well-being (eg being tired from staying up late viewing internet pornography)?

4. Are you preoccupied during the day with sexual fantasising based on images or experiences you have had on the internet?

5. Have you logged on to internet sex sites from your computer, through your mobile phone, PDA (personal digital assistant), smartphone or other handheld device?

6. Have you felt shame or depression following involvement with internet pornography?

7. Are you less involved with your spouse or close friends because of your involvement with pornography?

8. Have you lied, or sought to cover up from your spouse or others about your use of internet pornography?

9. Do you frequently become angry and irritable when asked by family or friends to decrease your involvement with the internet?

Answering 'Yes' to several of these suggests you may have a problem you need to talk to someone about. Freedom from recognised addictions like alcohol and drugs can take time and pornography use is no different.

The Cycle of Addiction

Addiction is set up in disconnectness and healed by being in connection again with others. When people feel disconnected and lonely they can be more vulnerable to what triggers their addiction. They will look to their addictions for comfort.

Most addicts have more than one addiction – some stronger than others. Addictions can be to substances, sex, food, exercise, work, gambling, games etc. If we have substance addictions (alcohol, drugs) these need to be treated first as they prevent us from working on other addictions.

Inwardly a whole series of things are happening: 'malaises' of loneliness, anger, fear, anxiety, boredom, fear of abandonment, fear of engulfment by other situations or people.

These can build up until they feel overwhelming. The addictive personality struggles to regulate them and does not know how to manage these feelings.

If people can identify the cycle of their addictive behaviour, then they can also identify exit strategies. These are 'alternative behaviours' that can be used to alleviate their malaises instead of the 'build-up behaviours'. The sooner these are substituted, the quicker an individual can escape the cycle. For example, an exit strategy might be to make a 'gratitude list', use physical exercise to change body chemistry, or social; do something to help reconnect to other human beings in a healthy way.

Identifying the destructive core beliefs – that whisper on the inside – and thinking of alternative constructive ones will be key to strengthening inner resources to break the cycle of addiction. For example: 'I'm bored and have achieved nothing today; therefore I have failed'. Alternatively: 'I have had a mellow day, filling in the gaps and recharging. Tomorrow I can achieve more.'

Problems arising from Pornography

Internet pornography can appear, at first, to promise freedom and some sexual excitement. Many testify that in the medium to long term, there is no freedom and that using pornography can lead to problems.

Effect on marital relationships

As a result of using pornography, a person's attitudes may

change and become distorted. For example, the individual may start regarding women merely as sex objects, or asking their partner to do the things they have seen whilst using pornography, even if they make her feel uncomfortable.

The comparison between the airbrushed, make-believe of online images and the individual's spouse can lead to a loss of sexual interest, sometimes making it difficult to ejaculate and maintain an erection.

Effect on family relationships
Someone using pornography can distance themselves from their spouse and children as they devote more and more time to the habit and its associated behaviours.

If an individual's pornography use is discovered by the family, it can have severe impacts on spouse and children (see chapters 4 and 5).

Drain on resources

As time goes on the person is likely to give increasing amounts of time, money and energy to gratify his desires and may have to resort to hiding the evidence. In extreme cases, an individual may lose his job if he is discovered using pornography at work, leading to financial difficulties for the user and his family.

Guilt and feelings of low self-esteem/separation from God

An individual can feel conflict about pornography: wanting to access it, but feeling awful when they do. They may not be meeting their own moral standards, but feel powerless to change.

Crimes

In extreme cases, use of pornography can lead to sexual violence against women and in others to accessing porno-graphic pictures of child abuse.

Chapter two
Finding Freedom

Part I
Choice and change

Any of us who has tried to keep to a diet or 'turn over a new leaf' knows how difficult it can be to change how we live – and keep to it. Deciding to turn away from something we recognise is wrong is challenging. We need an understanding of ourselves and of whatever it is we are trying to overcome. On top of that we must muster the strength to carry it out.

It's a process of:

* identifying our weakness
* making a decision to change
* working out how to do it
* getting the help we need to stick to it

How can things change?

Recognise that while sexual drive is natural, it can be indulged in a wrong way

As sex is a normal human drive it is neither surprising nor a sign of moral failure if an inappropriate sexual thought sometimes comes to mind. The problem arises if, rather than dismissing such a thought or desire, we focus and feed on it.

It all begins with the mind and eyes

'Temptation comes from our own desires, which entice us and drag us away. These desires give birth to sinful actions. And when sin is allowed to grow, it gives birth to death.' **(James 1:14-15)**

Given the visual nature of men, what we watch matters. What we think about matters too.

'…whatever is true, whatever is noble, whatever is right, whatever is pure, whatever is lovely, whatever is admirable. If anything is excellent or praiseworthy, think about such things.' **(Philippians 4:8)**

Someone once said that the most powerful sexual organ is the brain! If immoral thoughts are allowed to linger in the mind, these sexual fantasies and desires are encouraged. When this process is repeated continuously it becomes embedded in that person's life. There is an old proverb that goes like this:

> Sow a thought, and you reap a desire.
> Sow a desire and you reap an act.
> Sow an act and you reap a habit.
> Sow a habit and you reap a lifetime.

Anyone who is determined to stop accessing pornography must begin with what they see and what they think about.

'I have made a covenant with my eyes not to look lustfully at a girl'. **(Job 31:1)**

Choices

A really important part of being human is having the power to choose. Christians believe in a God who has set out the best ways to live, but does not *force* people to do what is right. Inevitably we all make bad choices and sometimes these lead to all kinds of complications, disappointments and pain. Christian faith involves coming to God humbly, confessing our failures and deciding before Him to turn away from what is wrong. The Bible says that we all need to ask God for forgiveness and we all need His help to be different. Taking this step can start us on a journey of hope towards 'living free'.

'If we claim that we're free of sin, we're only fooling our-selves. A claim like that is errant nonsense. On the other

hand, if we admit our sins—make a clean breast of them—
he won't let us down; he'll be true to himself. He'll forgive
our sins and purge us of all wrongdoing.'
(from The Message version of The Bible: 1 John 1:8,9)

God will forgive and restore

The Christian life is all about how God's mercy and grace helps us to achieve His standards of integrity. When we pray with honesty and sorrow about our failures and weaknesses and resolve to change, something amazing can happen. The Bible says that when we do this God forgives us totally and comes into our lives to change us from the inside out.

Damaged relationships can be restored

One of the first casualties of wrongdoing is the loss of people's trust in us. When a husband or wife discovers that their partner has had an affair, they feel their marriage relationship has been seriously threatened. Using pornography to feed sexual fantasy may be less far-reaching but it is still a betrayal – it is actually in the same category as an affair with a real person. *'But I tell you that anyone who looks at a woman lustfully has already committed adultery with her in his heart.'* **(Matt 5:28)**

Some men find it difficult to understand why pornography is so repugnant to their partners. 'What's the big deal?' they may say. Partners of people accessing pornography frequently feel cheapened and cheated. A wife may wonder who or what her husband is imagining when he makes love to her. She cannot compete with the seductive images he feasts his eyes on when he sits in front of the computer – and why would she ever want to anyway? 'When I looked at some of the stuff myself I felt physically sick,' one woman said. 'How could he allow himself to want that? Where does it leave our relationship and my dignity as the woman he married?'

Setting things right again will be less painful for them both if the injured party can try to understand the nature of pornography and be prepared to walk the path of forgiveness rather than to reject and condemn outright. This is by no means easy for either – but many couples have come through and found their relationships have not only been restored but also strengthened. However, this rarely happens without help.

Positive action for those affected

So, you recognise the need to give up pornography – how do you begin in practical terms?

The first step is to **make the decision that you will do whatever it takes** to bring about a change. There may be many reasons for reaching this point and if you are determined, the decision to change could result in a significant change. Pray and ask God for forgiveness. Ask that he would help you work through the practical changes you need to make.

Think about the *time of day* when the greatest struggle occurs

When are you most likely to give in to temptation in this area? Being vigilant and proactive makes it easier to resist. Asking someone who is aware of the problem if you can briefly contact them at that time may be an added help – and make all the difference.

Identify the *place* of struggle

Perhaps it is the office computer, mobile phone, handheld device or the internet at home. How can you be prepared so you do not succumb to the temptation?

Recognise where this behaviour is coming from

This is often helpful; the attraction of pornography some-times springs from the circumstances around past sexual experience. For others, it may be as a result of stress, depression, loneliness or difficult circumstances in their marriage. For still others it may be curiosity that got out of control when there is so much easy access to pornography at our fingertips.

Find some help

Part of the power of pornography is in its secrecy. If you decide you want to change, consider asking someone to walk with you through this change. You will break the power of secret sin. Consider who you could ask for support in this – a friend, a colleague, someone in leadership in your church? You may want someone to act as an accountability partner. You may ask for help from a trained counsellor, seek out a mentor or join a group of others affected in a similar way, so that you can support each other.

Practical resources

Take a look at the final chapter to find books, websites and other useful contacts. One of the most effective of these is www.covenanteyes.com which enables someone else (a friend or mentor or even a spouse) to be sent regular information about sites you have visited. Access via www.care.org.uk/anon for one free month.

Put some effective strategies in place

Practical steps with your computer/electronic devices

- Use accountability software which will tell others what you are watching. See chapter 6.

- Be accountable to others for your use of mobile phones and handheld devices that can connect to the internet, since, at the time of writing, accountability software is not yet available for these devices. Avoid going online using these devices.

- Download effective software to block unhelpful material from your computer.

- Delete all unhelpful material already on your computer and if necessary replace the hard drive. In addition, get rid of any pornographic material hidden in the house, garage, shed or work-place.

- Create a password or screensaver on your computer that motivates you to say 'no'. The name of your wife, mother, daughter or sister perhaps.

- Keep the door open when using the computer and have the screen facing the door so others can see what is on it. Keep your computer an 'open door' in regard to profiles, email addresses etc.

- Be wise about whether it is the best idea to access the computer when alone.

Practical steps with your thoughts

- Have a 'virtual screensaver' that kicks in on the computer screen of your mind as soon as any erotic or unhelpful thought or image appears there. This could be a mental picture of someone you would never wish to hurt and offend (eg spouse).

- Find a phrase which inspires and encourages, write it on a small card to memorise and repeat frequently - especially in those moments of temptation. A Christian can remind himself: *'The temptations in your life are no different from what others experience. And God is faithful. He will not allow the temptation to be more than you can stand. When you are tempted, he will show you a way out so that you can endure.'*

(from The Message version of The Bible – 1 Corinthians 10:13)

Practical steps with your behaviour

- Change your patterns of behaviour - you know when *you* are most in danger - and devise strategies to take you away from the situation or to give you alternative activities.

- If you are more vulnerable when you drink alcohol, consider giving it up or being extremely careful when and where you drink.

- If your wife goes out regularly one evening of the week, consider forming a men's group to meet at the same time in your house – but no computer activity that night!
- Read *Every Man's Battle* and *Searching for Intimacy* (see final chapter for details)

Practical steps with spiritual life

- Develop your relationship with God by reading your Bible and praying each day – even just for a few minutes.
- When under pressure to give into temptation, audibly ask God for help, and then make a phone call to someone you trust.
- Connect with other Christians socially as well as in church.
- If appropriate, spend time each day, praying with your wife. Register with www.when2pray.net which sends weekly emails that help you to do this.

Practical steps with relationships

- Develop an accountability relationship with another Christian man (or woman, as appropriate), or join a Christian support group of other individuals working through these issues.
- Develop openness and honesty with your wife, girlfriend or fiancée.
- Consider going on a marriage enrichment course. Look at www.themarriagecourse.org to find a course near you.
- Try to go to bed at the same time as your wife.

Part II
Finding a mentor

As well as asking God to give you the strength you need, it will make an enormous difference to find someone who is willing to give moral, practical and spiritual support. Being accountable to another person makes positive change much more likely. However, be realistic about how far someone else can help you. It might be tempting to lean on them too much – *you* are the one who will need to work the most on overcoming your difficulty. The mentor is there to help, not take on the weight of it themselves.

Some feel they couldn't possibly tell another person – for what would they think? Be encouraged! Others' experience confirms again and again that opening up to another person is a relief because they are likely to offer genuine understanding, compassion and want to help. It also breaks the power of secret sin.

The next step is deciding to find that person, asking to be accountable to him. It is a good idea to pray for wisdom and guidance as you think about who might be a suitable mentor. It should be someone you look up to and respect, someone mature, trustworthy, compassionate and a good listener – and, most importantly, someone who believes in the importance of 'living free'.

Now you can approach the potential mentor to ask if you could meet on a regular basis, so you can be accountable to him and receive help with your spiritual journey. If he is willing, take the opportunity to be honest and talk through any struggles with pornography right at the start.

The first meeting

Eating and drinking together in a neutral place is helpful. During this first meeting check he is still willing to take on this mentoring role. The difficulties with pornography should definitely be explained by this stage. Be brave and don't hold back the truth or cover up the extent of your problem; it is easier to put it all on the table at the beginning. One key to the success of this mentoring relationship will be your honesty. Another is not to have unrealistic expectations about how much the mentor can support you, for instance, expecting him to be constantly available on the phone or able to meet more often than you have agreed.

Discuss how often you would like to meet and where. Initially suggest meeting once a week for about an hour, at a time and place that suits him. Remember, *he* is helping *you*, so try to fit in with his schedule. As time progresses the meetings should happen less often.

Discuss the structure of the meetings. Following conversation at a social level, it can be useful to have an agreed set of questions which the mentor asks. These should be chosen to open up useful areas for discussion.

Ask how he feels about being contacted by phone if you are experiencing a particularly tough time. If he agrees to this be very careful not to abuse this freedom.

Try to arrange the next mentoring session before parting. Otherwise, gaps in between can lengthen; and eventually meetings may stop altogether. This is one of the main reasons why some accountability/mentoring relationships fail.

Mutual support

It is not unknown for one man to approach another for help only to find that both of them struggle with the same difficulties. If this is the case then most of the advice in this book still holds true, but if a potential mentor is still experiencing serious struggles then he should seek help for himself. An alternative is to split meetings into two with each one asking the other their agreed questions and each encouraging the other. This is more difficult but some have found it successful.

The other option is for each to find someone else to help them.

As meetings continue

There is no absolute formula as it depends upon your personalities and how the situation develops.

As a trusting relationship develops, expect to be asked more probing personal questions.

It is good to pray together – perhaps with your eyes open if you are in a public place. Make sure to keep praying during the week and, if a crisis arises, contact your mentor so you can pray together over the phone, as this can help enormously in the face of temptation.

Chapter three
Offering Support

Part I
Being a Christian mentor

Today pornography is more easily accessed than ever before. Some men – and a growing number of women – are using pornography occasionally, others use it more regularly and some would consider themselves addicted. How can they be helped?

Perhaps you are a church leader, a counsellor or just a friend to whom someone has come and opened up about personal struggles with internet pornography. You may be reading this book because that is exactly what has happened to you, or maybe you are trying to be prepared just in case.

Am I the right person to help?
If a person comes to you, you need to consider how involved you can be. People seeking to overcome inappropriate sexual habits and addictions tend to respond well to accountability, but you need to be realistic about how much time and energy you can give. Could you offer to be a software accountability partner? Can you be a more in-depth mentor or do you need to refer them to someone else who may be better able to help them?

Being an effective mentor

What does it mean to be a mentor?
The Oxford English Dictionary defines a mentor as 'an experienced and trusted advisor'. The New Testament describes what he or she does as 'discipling', helping someone to learn to follow God more closely and increasingly lead a holy life. A mentor is not the same as a counsellor or therapist; the role is more of a listening friend who suggests ways forward, offering some emotional and spiritual support.

Here, we are considering the mentoring of someone who is struggling with a particular weakness. It is important to be open, honest and real in the relationship. Share about yourself if you think it will directly help your friend or help the relationship, but avoid presenting yourself either as an expert with all the answers, or someone who has not yet learned to overcome temptation himself.

The relationship will exist for a clear purpose, so you will need to agree necessary boundaries to help achieve the agreed aims.

How can a mentoring relationship help?

It should have these characteristics:

1. Based on **acceptance** of and belief in the person.

2. Involve **regular contact but not** an overdependence on the mentor's support.

3. Include time for **caring questions** that will help the person to give honest answers.

4. Be conducted with a **wise understanding** of the situation – but not condoning wrong actions.

5. Be characterised by **confidentiality and accountability** without condemnation or rejection. You both need to agree on the rules of this relationship.

6. Feature **support and encouragement** as the person tries to make significant changes and overcome sexual struggles.

7. Provide **practical advice and strategies** to resist the temptation to access pornography.

8. Focus on **Biblical truth** and practical remedies more that on a personal weakness.

9. Be supported by **prayer** – both when you are together, and in-between meetings. Commit yourself to pray regularly about this relationship and ask for Christ's presence within to guide and prompt you.

A mentor's responsibilities

- **Be sure that it is right** for you to undertake this mentoring relationship and that you are doing it from choice not under emotional pressure from your friend. Your responsibility for this other person is limited – it is his life and only he can take the decisions necessary to become free of addiction.

- Your role is to **help him on his spiritual journey**, step by step. Asking questions that uncover hidden issues and stimulate thought is often very effective. Sometimes you will be able to offer wise advice, but it is often better to help your friend work out solutions to problems with minimal guidance.

- At the outset be clear about the **parameters of this relationship**. Write these down and if the situation changes refer to them, perhaps calling on the help of a third impartial person if difficulties arise. A good test of the relationship is to ask 'which of us is working harder on breaking this addiction?' The answer should always be, the person seeking help.

- It is important to gain permission to address difficult questions and then keep asking them. **Do not be shy to challenge the person** even if they seem to be keeping their distance; this could be as a result of shame, feeling unworthy and not wanting to waste your time.

- It is useful to **keep notes**, but these should be basic and written so they make little sense to anyone else who might find them. Keep them safe and when the mentoring relationship finishes, dispose of them, telling your friend that you have done this.

- You may **consider informing your or his church leader**. There are a number of issues here. If the man you are mentoring is in leadership or in some other position where his behaviour could damage the church there are strong grounds to confide in the pastor/minister. However, if you do talk about the person, you must make sure he knows what is being said and to whom.

- **Protect yourself from the 'dynamic of transference'** – listening empathetically to his struggles may have a negative effect on your own thought life. At the end of each session, be careful to pray. Try not to dwell on any anxiety you may feel in between meetings.

- **Be careful not to express too much interest in the details** of the struggle rather than focusing on any progress. Asking about the details of some misadventure may be unnecessary or even unhelpful to either of you. Ask yourself, 'Is knowing this in the person's best interests or am I asking to satisfy my own curiosity?' There is a danger of being titillated by someone's sexual stories. If this happens it is not a reason to stop helping them but a challenge to **practise what we preach in terms of self-control.**

Managing a mentoring relationship

There are a number of practicalities to decide upon when mentoring someone. Each case is different, but the following questions and answers may be helpful.

How long should it last?

That's up to you. Right at the start you could both put a date in your diary, say six weeks or three months away, when you will discuss the success of the relationship and each have the freedom to withdraw or meet for another three months. It is a good idea to set a time limit and discuss how to end when that day comes in a way that will not leave the person feeling abandoned. It is much easier to have this conversation at the outset – you can refer to it in subsequent meetings, especially as the time limit approaches.

How often will we make contact?

At first, it is helpful to see each other for about an hour once a week, then fortnightly, until you agree it will be enough to meet less frequently. It is part of your role as the mentor to gauge this. It is good to agree a time limit and have a plan as to how you will bring the meetings to an end. Most importantly, **be realistic as to what you can and cannot offer**. Don't create expectations that you cannot sustain long-term.

During the early weeks your friend may ask to be in touch perhaps by phone for encouragement and prayer when he faces temptations, but you must be clear about how often you are willing for him to do this.

It could be that the person you are helping starts to become controlling. His problem involves addictive thoughts and behaviour and you need to be aware of the possibility that he will 'get addicted' to relying on you!

What happens at the first meeting?

You have agreed to a mentoring relationship and you are meeting up for the first time. You might want to meet over a coffee or a meal as this creates a more relaxed atmosphere.

Make it clear that you expect him to open up in response to the direct questions you will ask. While your attitude will be gentle and understanding that this is not easy, you should not have to prise the truth out of him.

If you have not resolved practical issues like how often you will meet, you should do so at this meeting. Explain how you reckon the relationship will work, discuss and write down the expectations you both have and then pray together.

Arrange the next meeting and agree that both of you will spend time thinking if this 'accountability' relationship should continue.

What next?

If both are still willing to continue, on the second meeting you should:

- Start at a social level, catching up on what each is doing.

- Suggest he chooses a Bible verse that has been helpful in his struggles to look at together when you next meet. Bringing Bible verses into the session will help you both keep God central to the conversation.

- Encourage the person to be honest with himself and explore ways to manage temptation. Discuss the practical strategies set out in chapter two, like blocking unsuitable material from the person's computer and installing accountability software. Help him to think about alternative healthy coping strategies when confronted with problem situations and encourage him to envisage practising them when this happens.

- Put together a framework of questions covering the points you need to consider. Although initially it might seem slightly artificial, these questions help to focus and remind you both of the reason for meeting – especially important as time goes by and the relationship becomes more relaxed and informal. Read these before every meeting as you pray for wisdom. As the mentor, you may sometimes wish to change these, but check that your friend is happy with that.

The following questions are a good framework to start a discussion. You should note any changes you both think would make them more useful. Once the questions are agreed, each should keep a copy.

General

1. Tell me about a highpoint and a disappointment in the past week.

2. What did you agree to do when we last met? How successful have you been?

3. In what ways have you taken care of your body with rest, sleep, exercise and healthy eating?

4. Can you share any particular stress – at work, home, in your relationships?

5. What do you see as the goal(s) for the period we are meeting together?

6. How are these goals being fulfilled?

Spiritual

1. On a scale of 1-10 how would you rate your current spiritual walk?

2. In what way do you sense that God is speaking to you?

3. Are you aware of any specific answers to prayer?

4. How have you been obedient to God since we last met?

5. In what ways have you stepped out in faith since we last met?

6. Share about any situations or sense of failure on your part that has blocked your relationship with God? What can you learn from your 'non-successes' this week?

7. Describe something about time with God in Bible reading and prayer and say what it meant for you.

Purity

1. What instances of success did you experience this week in keeping your thought life pure?

2. If you were tempted to look at pornography, how did you overcome that?

3. Were there occasions when you gave in? What can be learned from them?

4. How can I pray for you in the area of sexual sin?

5. What could you put in place to protect you from it happening?

Relationships

1. How is your relationship with your wife, children, work colleagues, friends?

2. What could you do to improve these relationships?

3. What specific things are you praying about for these people?

Final Question

What else would you like to discuss next time?

As meetings continue

There is no absolute formula as it depends upon your personalities and on how the situation develops, but these points may help. Confidentiality and legalities are covered here:

- As a trusting relationship develops, you can pose more questions – usually much more valuable than giving answers and advice. Pray for discernment to know the right questions for each time.

- Review accountability software logs.

- Keeping a record of successes and milestones of progress that will encourage and build up both of you.

- Remind each other about agreed aims and, if appropriate, pray together.

- After an agreed time, review what has been achieved and the progress he has made. You may then decide to see each other less often, change the nature of your meetings or even extend them to become a small support group for others to join. Make sure that neither of you are stuck in this relationship wishing it had ended sooner. Honest appraisal is essential.

- This formal accountability relationship must end whenever it has served its purpose. You may want to continue meeting informally as friends. However, be warned, this can be a very difficult transition and is perhaps not a good idea. You may want to consider maintaining on-line contact through accountability software with the person.

Confidentiality

You should **always maintain strict standards of confidentiality.**

A breach of confidentiality would damage the relationship and destroy trust at a time when the person is seeking to be open and has feelings of shame, unworthiness and inferiority. This is a very sensitive area and not only will the person be incredibly hurt if they hear of their story being related back to them by others, but may never open up to anybody again.

Resist the temptation to talk to others about the person you are helping – although if you are in an accountability relationship yourself it may be good to let them know what you are taking on.

What to do if the person is accessing illegal material

There are very important exceptions to the rule of not passing on information about the person's problem. If you believe he has broken the law you are required to report this. At the outset of your relationship you should say something like this, *'Although I want you to feel able to confide in me about your struggles – you need to know that I can't maintain confidentiality if you confess to doing something that breaks the law. In that event I would be legally bound to inform the police.'*

There is a clear legal distinction between what is regarded as adult pornography and the 'indecent' images of children or child abuse material sometimes referred to as 'child pornography'. An individual who produces or downloads child pornography commits a **serious criminal offence**.

If you become aware this is happening, you should ideally, go together to tell the police about any offence. However, if that is not realistic then, under the Children's Act, **you have a duty of care, once you are party to the knowledge that a person is accessing child pornography. This means that you should immediately report what you know to the police.**

It will probably be necessary to do this without informing the person involved that you are doing so, otherwise they are likely to destroy the evidence before the police have a chance to act.

If he promises to inform the police by himself, be wary of believing this. Be aware that he may be calling your bluff to create himself an opportunity to destroy any evidence. You are dealing with a person with an addictive personality who is highly likely to act deceptively if he has to.

If you are unsure about the legality of the material an individual has been accessing, refer the person to a professional counsellor – there are some suggestions in following paragraphs. They will then get the help they need and those trained to do so will follow up any legal implications.

In cases where an individual has been downloading indecent images of children, there is a **huge impact on the rest of the family**. The individual will be placed on the Sex Offenders Register for a period of time (a minimum of two years up to a maximum of life). It is likely that Children's Social Care (Social Services) may also be involved with the family, and sometimes the Probation Service too.

Churches can help families going through this by adopting a contract outlining the support the church is providing along with any boundaries for the individual. Churches' Child Protection Advisory Service (CPAS) has pioneered contracts like these which have been used by many denominations successfully for many years. Details are in the chapter at the end of this book.

What to do if things don't improve

If the individual becomes evasive, seems unmotivated or too busy to return your calls, ask if they have changed their mind about being open and challenge them about it. This may help them re-engage with the problem and make a fresh resolve to face up to it. If you are experiencing difficulties with the relationship, discuss this with another trusted person. If possible let the person you are mentoring be aware of your concern and that *you* need support.

However, some men find that an accountability relationship with a mentor is not enough to help them to control their sexual behaviour. If you believe this to be true it is essential to tell him frankly that he needs additional help. This kind of support can be accessed in various ways. He could ask his GP to refer him to an addictions specialist therapist or make contact directly. The following websites will be helpful:

www.basrt.org.uk – British Association for Sexual and Relationship Therapy

www.ipm.org.uk – Institute of Psychosexual Medicine

The person may want to consider a 12-step programme, similar in structure to Alcoholics Anonymous. The following are links to groups operating in the UK. However, CARE cannot vouch for any of these groups.

www.sauk.org – Sexaholics Anonymous, meetings in UK

www.slaauk.org – Sex and Love Addicts Anonymous, meetings in UK

www.sexaa.org – Sex Addicts Anonymous, meetings in England and Scotland

www.saa-women.org – Sex Addicts Anonymous for women

Focusing on the person not the problem

Your response to the person needs to be sensitive, supportive and hopeful.

Condemnation on the one hand or over-identification on the other can leave the person – who is taking a huge risk by opening up and seeking help – without hope.

A listener can respond without passing judgement and, having heard the details, focus less on times of failure and more on occasions when the person resisted temptation. Conversations that explore good behaviour are usually more useful than those that dwell on weakness.

Remind the person about strategies that can keep the problem at bay (see Chapter 2, Part I). Some find that being alone in the evening causes temptations to increase – but something as simple as listening to favourite music may help them to say 'no' more easily.

Marriage and family relationships

When a person is struggling with internet pornography, ask them about their marriage or any other relationship.

- Is the person single, sexually frustrated in marriage, or going through a break up?

- Does the person's partner know about the problem? If so, how are they coping with it and do they need support too? Views differ, but some say it may not always be for the best for a man to confess sexual sin to his spouse; careful consideration is needed. For other spouses, the situation will be obvious.

- Check the history of the problem; does it predate the marriage or is it a recent development? Did he think using pornography was normal until challenged or before she found out? What in their individual pasts may have some influence on how things are now?

- Which one came first: internet use or lack of intimacy in marriage? Some users blame their marriage partner saying, 'I have to use this stuff, I've got no choice, because my wife isn't interested any more.' There may be marital or sexual difficulties but this is not a reason or excuse to use pornography. It will exacerbate the problem, not solve it. Marriage counselling can help the couple find new love and trust enabling them to meet one another's sexual and intimacy needs.

- Seeing the couple together may be helpful. (However, this is a very sensitive area and it could be better for a female partner to confide in another woman.) Inviting them both to say what they enjoy about the relationship is as important as asking about the difficulties. Listen to both of them rather than hear the story mainly from the more verbal or dominant partner – encouraging the other one to share may be a challenge. Let each express their true feelings and identify improvements they would like to see in the marriage before deciding what help they need. This may mean referral to a qualified family or couple therapist.

Mental health issues

You may become concerned that the person you are help-ing is showing signs of crossing over between imagination and reality. You could consider the following:

- Does the person know when they are 'imagining' in their head and when they are 'doing things' in reality? Are they in danger of acting out any of their pornography fantasies? These issues are important to check and if in doubt, as above, you should refer the person to a counsellor, family GP or other professional service for assessment.

- In such a case, do follow them up, checking that they have kept any agreed appointment and told the professional what they shared with you. If not, and you are concerned, particularly about the safety of children, contact social services or the police, having informed the person you are going to do so, because they have not attended.

Relationship with God

We need wisdom to help a person reach a place of responsibility and faithfulness in his relationship with God, himself and others. One of our roles as confidant is to wean the person from dependence on us into a close daily walk with their heavenly Father, knowing Christ's presence and aware of the Holy Spirit's guidance and power.

Part II:
Starting a Christian support group

You may have found help from a personal mentor and now want to help others. Or there may not be a suitable mentor available, but you know others who are going through the same difficulties as you. In these situations, starting a support group is often a helpful idea. On your own and isolated it is hard to change. When Christian men join together, share their struggles, plan their strategies and start to encourage and challenge each other, the situation changes.

> *'Therefore confess your sins to each other and pray for each other so that you may be healed'*
> **James 5:16**

Who should set up a group for men who are struggling?
If you are an individual wanting to be free from sexual sin, you may be just the person who should set up a group because you understand something of the battle, feel motivated to change, and perhaps would like to help others in a similar situation. Don't say: 'But I haven't found victory myself yet, how can I start a group?' Talk to someone you respect about this who may know of others who struggle with pornography and need encouragement and help.

Does a group need a leader?
It is tempting to think that a group of like-minded men all struggling with sexual addiction will not need a leader

as it can run in a sort of democratic way with, perhaps, a rotating facilitator. Often, experience shows that having a leader is a better option. He will be someone who can pray and plan each meeting, keeping things moving forward.

Why can't I just pray and ask God to deliver me from using pornography?

You should pray and ask for healing. For some their prayers will be answered immediately. For others, it will be a longer process of sanctification and healing for them and their families. The testimony of many is that they need to walk this road with others.

Is it too heavy to focus on this one issue?

Being involved in accessing pornography affects every area of life and prevents a person developing as they should. As group members tackle this one issue they usually find themselves needing to deal again with the very basics of their faith. Coming together and being honest with each other makes a difference. Individuals develop trust for one another, which make this a wonderful opportunity for friendships to develop.

'In our group the men found that their whole Christian life was transformed. As we faced this one issue we found ourselves looking for a consistent Christian life, because it is impossible to become pure without a revolution in our spiritual life. It soon became evident that we had to change from being "one-day a week Christians" to those who live out their faith on a daily basis. Our whole outlook needed to change and doing this together gave us the strength to keep going.'

Some practical suggestions

Running a group

Ideally, there should be material on what size group works, how long the meetings should be each time they meet and where this should be, what sort of time scale they should last, how to structure meetings and how to deal with confidentiality issues.

Why should we become pure?

This is a good question to start the meeting. Go round the group with each person giving a good reason for the importance of personal purity. It reinforces resolve and reminds everyone why they are part of the group. These reasons should become part of our 'arsenal' when temptations come. Typical reasons might be:

* If I am married; to fulfil my vow to be faithful to my wife.
* It will draw me closer to God.
* I want to know I am living a consistent Christian life.
* I want to grow and develop my Christian faith.
* Although impurity can be pleasurable, I know it damages my life.
* It will give me a happier sex life.

Being accountable

Part of the strength of a support group is to encourage accountability:

- **To God** – How much do we fear God? Many of us actually fear our sin being discovered by others more than we do it being seen and known by God. Taking seriously the fact that God sees our sexual sin should help us not to indulge in it.

- **To ourselves** – We owe it to be accountable to ourselves as a form of self-respect, caring about harming ourselves.

- **To others** – another person or the group. This must be by mutual agreement and can initially be voluntary as group members learn to trust each other. When this stage is reached, a chart like the one on p51 could be useful. It can be used to discuss progress towards individual goals, celebrating successes, praying and seeking forgiveness where someone has fallen short of their own expectations.

Ask each person to record at the end of each day how they are getting on. Initially this is to find out what we are really like, and to develop self-awareness. The next time you meet together, give them an opportunity to share their findings, so that honesty and full accountability are achieved.

Part of being accountable is **dealing with excuses**. We are all very good at making excuses for our behaviour. Talk together about the different excuses we may use, expose them and discuss them. How can we overcome them? A good exercise: how would you justify speeding in your car on a clear road? What are the parallels with taking risks sexually in your thought life and online activity?

Goals	M	T	W	T	F	S	S
I have not accessed internet pornography							
I have not fantasised sexually							
I have not deliberately looked through newspapers or magazines looking for sexual gratification							
I have not bought pornographic magazines, videos or DVDs							
I have not watched sexually explicit scenes on TV							
I have prayed today							
I have memorized a scripture today							
I have read and meditated in the Bible today							
I have worshipped God today							
(If married) I have shown appreciation for my wife today							
I have contacted one of my group to encourage them today							

Needing the Holy Spirit

Whilst the group is a key ingredient for men in overcoming sexual impurity in their lives, the ultimate goal is for the individuals in the group to stand alone with integrity and be enabled to fight their individual battles. Each individual needs to know the reality of God's empowerment to help everyone live free.

'That he would... make you realise the magnificence and splendour of the inheritance promised to Christians – and how tremendous is the power available to us who believe in God ... the same divine energy which was demonstrated in Christ when he raised him from the dead!'
Ephesians 1:18 (JB Phillips)

Hallmarks of a successful group

- **Honest, real and open.** It is important for the men to be straightforward in their discussion. No hiding.

- **Positive attitude.** Drawing out and celebrating successes as they occur.

- **Focused.** Consider reading *Every Man's Battle* with study guide already mentioned. (see Further Resources)

- **With a sense of moving forward.** There will be steps backward but keep a sense of hope and expectation for future success.

- **Challenging.** Be tough on each other in the context of understanding and support.

- **Supportive.** Help each other cope with key times and situations when temptations occur.

- **Strategic.** Work together on ways to overcome this problem.

- **Radical.** The mind must be renewed with new thinking habits.

- **Grounded in scripture.** There are a couple of Bible

Study outlines following. Many groups choose a weekly verse to memorise. Biblical truth needs to work its way into our hearts to be ready for us to bring to mind in times of temptation or discouragement. Sharing these with others is a great help, quite a challenge but worth the effort.

* **Prayer-centred.** Confession, prayer and thanksgiving. Use CARE's resource *Purify*, a CD journey of reflection through music, Bible verses and prayers.

Two character studies from the Bible

David and Joseph in their encounters with sexual temptation.

READ:
2 Samuel 11: 1-5

'In the spring of the year, when kings normally go out to war, David sent Joab and the Israelite army to fight the Ammonites. They destroyed the Ammonite army and laid siege to the city of Rabbah. However, David stayed behind in Jerusalem. Late one afternoon, after his midday rest, David got out of bed and was walking on the roof of the palace. As he looked out over the city, he noticed a woman of unusual beauty taking a bath. He sent someone to find out who she was, and he was told, "She is Bathsheba, the daughter of Eliam and the wife of Uriah the Hittite." Then David sent messengers to get her; and when she came to the palace, he slept with her. She had just completed the purification rites after having her menstrual period. Then she returned home. Later, when Bathsheba discovered that she was pregnant, she sent David a message, saying, 'I'm pregnant.' (The story continues in verses 6-27)

Genesis 39: 6b-12

'Joseph was a very handsome and well-built young man, and Potiphar's wife soon began to look at him lustfully. "Come and sleep with me," she demanded. But Joseph refused. "Look," he told her, "my master trusts me with everything in his entire household. No one here has more authority than I do. He has held back nothing from me except you, because you are his wife. How could I do such a wicked thing? It would be a great sin against God." She kept putting pressure on Joseph day after day, but he refused to sleep with her, and he kept out of her way as much as possible. One day, however, no one else was around when he went in to do his work. She came and grabbed him by his cloak, demanding, "Come on, sleep with me!" Joseph tore himself away, but he left his cloak in her hand as he ran from the house.'

David was in the wrong place at the wrong time; as the king he should at that time of year have been accompanying his army and fighting the enemy. Instead, he was still in Jerusalem where, unable to sleep one night, he observed from his roof terrace a beautiful woman bathing. He enquired after her, and although he discovered she was someone else's wife, still sent for her and had sex with her.

Joseph, on the other hand, seemed to have prepared a variety of mental arguments and when the moment of temptation came he put them into practice. He was apparently a young man of about 17 or 18, (see beginning of the story in Genesis 37:2) far from home in a strange land, but…

- He did not take advantage of this woman
- He honoured her marriage vows even though she may not have regarded them

- He honoured his own marriage vows, even though he hadn't made them yet

- He respected God's view on adultery, considering it to be morally wrong

- He explained his view to her and did his best to avoid her on a daily basis. Then, when all else failed, he ran!

Points to consider

- Compare David with Uriah – Bathsheba's husband (read verses 6-13). He was a man with spiritual backbone and inner strength. Even though he knew that his 'brothers-in-arms' were going without sexual pleasure because of the war, he resisted the opportunity of a pleasant evening in the arms of his wife. What gave him the power to resist? He wasn't a man alone fighting his own battles but was part of an army. He took strength from being part of that group, strongly identifying with them and showing admirable self-control – it is not likely that anyone would have thought the worse of him for going to his wife. It seems that in this matter of sexual purity Uriah was head and shoulders above his king.

- There are a number of boundaries, moments or choices in this account where David could have halted, but at each point he continued down the slippery slope. David 'crossed the line' in his head, long before he had Bathsheba in his arms.

- When you think about Joseph, how many men that you know would take that sort of evasive action under similar circumstances? Clearly Uriah was walking close to God and had the fear of the Lord well established in his life. He was unlikely to have been lying awake at night fantasising about this woman. He kept short accounts with his thoughts and eyes.

Questions to discuss:

1. Consider the ripple effect from the action of each of these men

2. What can we learn from Joseph's example?

3. Having considered David's lack of wisdom and self-control, compared with Joseph's attitude and actions, how would you describe your strategy for avoiding immorality?

4. To what extent do you think it is true to say that we 'cross the line' in our heads, long before we take action?

Chapter four

For Better, For Worse

- from a wife's point of view

> " *Can my Christian husband really be into this stuff?* "

This can be the sort of reaction when a woman finds her partner is using pornography for sexual stimulation. Others will be far too aware of pornography, being asked to watch pornographic videos/DVDs or look at magazines before any marital sex act.

You may be a wife who is suspicious that something is wrong. Perhaps you are experiencing some of the following with your spouse:

- Preoccupation with looking at the opposite sex or other visual, sexual stimuli.

- Insisting on his own internet account and e-mail address.

- Unexplained credit card bills (or having a separate credit card that only one spouse uses).

- Unexplained absences or patterns of late night working, especially when the reasons given are inconsistent.

- Staying up late, after everyone has gone to bed, so he can log onto the internet privately.

- Emotional and spiritual distance between the two of you.

- Sudden increase in demands for sex, especially sexual practices that make you uncomfortable.

- Sudden decrease in interest in sex. If your spouse is channelling all his sexual energy into pornography, he may exhibit low or no interest in physical intimacy within your marriage.

- A sense that your spouse is 'not there' mentally and emotionally during lovemaking.

- Increase in moodiness, anger and harsh blaming.

If you are, he might be using pornography. Consider discussing your concerns with your spouse in a calm, non-accusatory manner. If your concerns persist, talk to your pastor/vicar or a friend you can trust.

If you have discovered that your husband has been using internet pornography, your reaction will include a whole range of emotions and questions. There are many similarities here with other problems – alcohol, drug and gambling addictions or a 'flesh-and-blood' affair.

How are *you* feeling? Maybe.....

- *Disbelief* – 'is this the man I married?'

- *Anger* – 'how dare he betray me?'

- *Fear* – 'what is going to happen? Is there more that I don't know about? Is he engaged in other illicit sexual activities too?'

- *Blind panic* – 'what do I do? It's all crumbling around me.'

- *Loneliness* – 'no-one else will have gone through this. I can't tell anyone, they wouldn't understand and they'd look down on us both.'

- *Exhaustion* – 'this is going on for so long. I cannot relax or trust him.'

- *Guilt* – 'it's my fault that my husband is seeking satisfaction elsewhere.'

- *A sense of uselessness, worthlessness, failure* – 'his pornography devalues our love – what does he think of me? How could I have been so stupid and naive not to realise?'

- *Loss of libido* – 'who or what is he imagining when we make love? Sex makes me feel contaminated now.'

All these emotions are perfectly normal. It is natural to feel like this ... and please remember, you are not alone.

This is not an easy issue to raise with anyone. You may have a strong desire to share what you have discovered or, on the other hand, the thought of confiding in someone may feel almost impossible. If you can find a mature person who will be sympathetic, not unhelpfully shocked and ready to listen, you will probably find telling your story an enormous relief.

Remember that however isolated you may feel in your situation, there are increasing numbers of men (and many women too) who have become trapped in the web of internet and other pornography – many of them married. Again, you are not alone. God cares about you passionately and longs to draw closer to you at this time of emotional turmoil.

It's not your fault

Women can be very 'good' at guilt and tend to think that anything that goes wrong must be because of something they have or haven't done! Using pornography is *his choice*; it's not your fault. You are not responsible for his decisions and actions.

There may need to be some understanding about the nature and context of internet pornography and there may be things about your relationship you need to work on, for instance: whether you are willing to share intimately with him, how you encourage and build him up, how much interest and concern you express. But even as you recognise areas of neglect or lack of understanding in yourself and accept the need to change, this is absolutely no excuse for what he is doing.

Regardless of whether other men do this; if you are uncomfortable, it is wrong

It is reasonable to object and feel betrayed, although this may not be clear to your husband. One man said 'Why the fuss? It doesn't hurt anyone – it's not about you and me.' Another remarked, 'It would have been OK if you hadn't found out.' A great deal of listening, understanding, apologising and forgiving will be needed; things to be worked on from both sides of the relationship.

You are important and a precious individual

Even if you are feeling belittled and experiencing other negative emotions you need to remember your worth – to others and to God. This situation does not have to be taken by you as a slight on your sexuality. Remember you have choices abut how you react.

If after a while, he doesn't make steps to change he may need the shock of 'tough love'

The risk of losing something he values like the confidence of his children or the continuing of the marriage can help him face the pain of giving up his addiction. You should speak to your pastor and a lawyer before discussing separation.

So what can you do now?

- **Draw a line** in the sand and say 'enough is enough'. Don't ignore unacceptable behaviour, it will only get worse.

- **Be honest** with your husband about how you feel. This will take a while, it should not all be said at once, and some of what you share may be easier in a letter. The recovery process for you both will probably take some time.

- **Seek support** for you to survive the 'crazy time' of initial emotional response. Don't deny the pain or be super-spiritual about it. Consider talking to someone you know will be **understanding and share spiritual as well as practical insight.**

- **Protect your children** from exposure to pornography (see resources in Chapter 6).

Then

- Begin the journey of emotional healing and spiritual renewal. **Work towards complete forgiveness**. Give yourself space to be angry. Suppressed anger ends up with depression problems.

- **Read** *An Affair of the Mind* by Laurie Hall, and *Living with Your Husband's Secret Wars* by Marsha Means.

- **Read** the Help and Advice section on

www.care.org.uk/anon which has downloadable pages on help and support, including a section for wives and a confidential email address: anon@care.org.uk

- **Stand by your husband** as he tries to change. Don't try to change him yourself – it won't work! Encourage him to find the people and software resources that will help him. Consider being his accountability partner if that would work for you both. Pray for him regularly.

Recognise that there are many other Christian women who have been or are still in this situation. Seek out others who are walking the same path for mutual encouragement. Ask them to pray for you. Again, the wives section of the www.care.org.uk/anon website might help here.

Next

Continue the journey of emotional healing and spiritual renewal.

- Grieve what has been lost. We all react differently and so you may not be impacted in the same way as someone else by what has been revealed. You may though, feel some of the following losses about the relationship you thought you had: confidence and trust, security, sense of dignity and self-worth. Identify the hope you still have and see what can be salvaged and strengthened in this marriage.

- Gradually work out what it will mean to rebuild trust.

- Face up to the existence of any feelings of resentment, fear and anger you may have towards your spouse.

- Pray for wisdom, patience, love and hope especially as you deal with the negative emotions.
- If necessary, find a trusted counsellor to help you repair your damaged self esteem.

Work on your own character and be honest about any areas you need to change that God reveals to you.

Consider attending a course or counselling together to enrich and strengthen your marriage. See chapter 6 for suggestions.

Still later
Continue work towards authentic forgiveness – Read *Total Forgiveness* and *Totally Forgiving Ourselves* by Dr RT Kendall. Continue to work on your own character and conduct. Check the boundaries you have put in place are working. Rebuild your love relationship with your husband.Deepen your dependence on God

For a long time
You may need to work with a counsellor as a couple to restore trust, mutual caring and healthy decision-making. There will also be ongoing issues that may affect your children, friends, neighbours and other areas of your lives, including your church fellowship.

Remember that although the pain may take time to fade, many marriages can be restored and be stronger than ever.

Chapter five
Protecting Children

In today's highly sexualised society, even young children are bombarded by inappropriate images and innuendos from billboards in the street, magazine covers displayed in shops, on television, through music, printed material and on the computer. When it comes to mobile phones and computers, in most cases children know more about new technology than their parents.

Young people are connected in a digital world – to the internet and to each other via mobile phones, blogging, instant messaging, online gambling and social networking sites. This brings a whole new dimension of creativity and opportunities, but also risks exposure to pornography, to individuals who may chat to them inappropriately or try to meet them for sexual activity. Parents, teachers and children need to be internet 'aware' and understand how to be safe. We need to be wise and educate children about both the joys of using Information Communication Technology (ICT) and its dangers.

Young people downloading pornographic images

Fact: juveniles commit 30 per cent of sexual offences.

Today's media, especially popular music, declares the thrills of casual sex. Adolescents must navigate this cultural morass just at a time when hormonal surges and emerging feelings are making life confusing enough. Add to this mix the powerful effects of peer pressure, and it is understandable that many Christian teens have difficulties in pursuing sexual purity and God-honouring relationships. As stated earlier, the internet allows for easy access to pornographic images, both video and still. Where once young people were protected from gaining access to pornography, now it is just a click away, sometimes reached quite unwittingly.

Internet and stranger danger

There is little doubt that the internet has increased the risk of strangers contacting children.
'Safer Children in a Digital World, The Report of the Byron Review', 2008.

The internet is an excellent and effective learning and communication tool. Unfortunately there are unscrupulous individuals who use it to gain access to exploit and harm children. In considering the risks to children the above quote should hold strong resonance to all those wishing to protect children.

For many years child protection agencies have been educating the public about child abuse. There has been a need to dispel the myth of 'stranger danger' as in reality the majority of cases involve children being abused by those known to them, including parents, other family members, and also those in authority – teachers in schools and within a church context, youth workers and ministers of religion.

Now we need to revise our understanding and recognise that with the internet young people do need to under-stand 'stranger danger'. The internet allows for an individual to pretend to be someone they're not. There have been many instances of a sexual offender entering an online chat room pretending to be a child or teenager, and then sending emails and instant messages gaining the trust of the child (this is known as 'grooming') and then attempting to meet them in the real world. A young person may think they are communicating with a 14-year old girl when actually the person is a 40-year-old male. The older person may also seek to obtain live pictures of the young person if they have a web camera attached to their computer.

What can parents do to help their children?

- Consult organisations like Childnet International's 'Know it All': www.childnet.com/kia – and the Child Exploitation and Online Protection Centre's site, www.thinkuknow.co.uk

- Discuss what you believe are appropriate things for your children to use the internet for and encourage positive use

- Take an interest in what your child looks at, reads and does on any computer, including those belonging to friends and at school etc

- Consider moving your family computer to the living room so you can see what your child is doing

- Install blocking/filtering/accountability software

- Encourage your children to tell you about any online activities or conversations that make them feel uncomfortable

- Remind your children not to give out any personal information or meet someone they do not know without you being present

- If you suspect inappropriate chat or behaviour with your child online, you should discuss it with them and report to it the Child Exploitation and Online Protection Centre. You can make a report on their website, www.ceop.gov.uk

- If you have a concern about illegal or harmful content on the web, contact the Internet Watch Foundation – www.iwf.org.uk – they will want to know of any concerns about child sexual abuse images hosted anywhere in the world and criminally obscene content hosted in the UK

- Take time to talk to your child about sex, sexual relationships and pornography

Parents also need to remember that legislation does not draw a distinction between whether an adult or a young person downloads indecent images of children. A young person may prefer to download images of those they believe look like their peers, possibly under-age, and would be committing a criminal offence.

When children are exposed to pornography use in their family

When a member of the family is accessing pornography children are even more vulnerable – they may come across pornographic material stored on a home computer or walk in on the person as they view online and see what is on the screen. It is especially painful when this happens in a Christian family; those affected feel particularly shocked and betrayed. They have lost trust in the parent they thought was a hero, a good and godly example.

Some of the feelings and effects

- Frightened – scared
- Can't forget the pictures or lose them from their mind
- The adrenalin rush will bring distressing feelings with it
- Confusion and physical or psychological effects
- Aggression, difficulty sleeping, nightmares
- Corruption of their view of boy and girlfriends
- Increased interest in sex that is not normal

How to help

- Give space for the child or young person to talk
- Don't let yourself show shock
- Take it seriously

- Don't give a quick answer like 'You'll understand when you're older'
- Try not to blame anyone; however they came across this material
- Give them reassurance, eg, 'It isn't your fault'
- Accept their feelings, eg, 'It's OK to feel sad, angry or confused'
- Assure them that you are glad they came to you to talk about it
- If signs of trauma persist, get some professional help for your child
- Don't over react by not allowing them to use the computer at all but consider possible safeguards

In future, try to keep open lines of communication in the family; there will probably be an ongoing need to discuss these issues further.

Where to go for advice and help if child abuse has occurred

If there has been physical, sexual or emotional abuse within the family or another situation you know about, it is important that you get professional help, either from the police, Social Services or through The Churches' Child Protection Advisory Service (CCPAS). CCPAS offer a 24-hour telephone helpline [0845 120 4550] for places of worship and organisations with any child protection concerns, be they on- or off-line. Their website also has a 'Report Abuse' button link to the Child Exploitation and Online Protection (CEOP) Centre as a partner agency.

You will find a comprehensive list of these and other helpful agencies and resources in the next section.

Chapter 6
Further
Resources

We hope that the material and resources mentioned in this book will be of use and encouragement. Please contact us at CARE via anon@care.org.uk if you know of more resources that have helped you and could help others. Please note that the books and websites listed below are both UK and USA based.

Publications

Searching for Intimacy, ed. Lyndon Bowring. Authentic 2005
Addresses the sensitive issues surrounding internet pornography from a Christian standpoint.

Every Man's Battle: Winning the War on Sexual Temptation One Victory at a Time, Stephen Arterburn and Fred Stoeker. Waterbrook Press 2000
Goes straight for the jugular and tackles the major issues in a direct and unflinching manner.

'Help for the Sexually Desperate' *Christianity Today* article, March 2008 (USA)
Access from www.christianitytoday.com/ct/archives

Healing the Wounds of Sexual Addiction Dr Mark Laaser. Faithful and True Ministries 2004
Help for men and women caught in sexual addiction's downward spiral.

Shattered Vows Debra Laaser. Faithful and True Ministries 2008
Practical help for spouses of those struggling with sex addiction based on writer's own experiences.

The Silent War: Ministering to Those Trapped in the Deception of Pornography Henry J Rogers. New Leaf Press 2000
Writer's own story of addiction and how God helped him overcome it. Concrete steps for guiding others to climb out of, or avoid pornography's pit.

An Affair of the Mind Laurie Hall. Focus on the Family book published by Tyndale House Publishers, updated 2003
The experience of a woman who struggled with her husband's pornography addiction.

Living with Your Husband's Secret Wars Marsha Means. Revell 1999
Step by step help to find recovery and peace for any woman recovering from a relationship damaged by her husband's secret sins or sexual addiction.

Every Woman's Battle: Discovering God's Plan for Sexual and Emotional Fulfilment Stephen Arterburn and Shannon Ethridge. Waterbrook Press 2003
Spiritual direction and practical steps for developing healthy, fulfilling sexual and emotional intimacy.

Total Forgiveness Dr RT Kendall. Charisma House 2002 and *Totally Forgiving Ourselves* Dr RT Kendall.
Hodder and Stoughton 2008
Biblical and practical pointers to help you experience the incredible freedom found in total forgiveness.

Untangling the Web: Breaking Free from Sex, Pornography, and the Fantasy in the internet Age Robert Weiss and Jennifer Schneider, Alyson Publications Inc 2006
A non-Christian look at the developments on internet pornography usage and some of the strategies for breaking free.

Purify CD featuring Graham Kendrick, Lyndon Bowring and others. CARE 2006
Music, Bible verses and prayers leading listeners to find God's promise of forgiveness and restoration.

Websites

www.care.org.uk/anon – **CARE's website on the misuse of the internet.**

www.accountable2you.com – **free accountability software with additional options for a fee, including filtering software.**

www.ceop.gov.uk – **Child Exploitation and Online Protection Centre; providing internet safety advice for parents and carers and delivering a virtual police station for reporting abuse on the internet.**

www.childnet.com – **Up-to-date information for children, parents and teachers, including the Know It All suite of resources.**

www.covenanteyes.com – a service which tracks a person's web use and sends a report of all the sites visited to an 'accountability friend'. Tailor-made for each person, so that the accountability partner holds the key words and access. Free for first month via www.care.org.uk/anon – Covenant Eyes also provides filtering software.

www.ccpas.co.uk – Churches' Child Protection Advisory Service providing professional training, resources and support in areas of child protection. Helpline 0845 120 4550.

www.cvmen.org.uk – Christian Vision for Men; equipping the church to introduce every man in the UK to Jesus Christ.

www.integrity.com – filtering software for the family.

www.iwf.org.uk – use this website to report material that depicts child sexual abuse or other illegal material. Hotline 01223 237700.

www.kidsmart.org.uk – helps parents and children to get the most out of the internet.

www.mediawatchuk.org.uk – includes a section on children and the media, with advice on how best to protect children and respond to harmful influences in the media.

www.stopitnow.org.uk – A public information and awareness raising campaign regarding child sexual abuse.

www.themarriagecourse.org – preparation for engaged couples and marriage enrichment. Information on their website of nationwide courses.

www.thinkuknow.co.uk – website for young people, parents and teachers giving information and support.

www.when2pray.net – weekly e-prayers for married couples.

Support agencies

www.acc-uk.org – **Association of Christian Counsellors. Lists of accredited counsellors nationwide.**

www.basrt.org.uk – **British Association for Sexual and Relationship Therapy, lists therapists' details nationwide.**

www.ipm.org.uk – **Institute of Psychosexual Medicine.**

www.living-waters-uk.org – **sexual and relationship counselling.**

www.operationintegrity.org – **supports individuals struggling with sexual addiction; based in the USA.**

www.purelifeministries.org – **ministry 'leading Christians to victory over sexual sin and into a deeper life in God'; based in the USA.**

www.purewarrior.org – **dedicated to rescuing men from the grip of secret sexual sin, and restoring and training them in Christian sexual purity; based in the USA.**

www.sexaddict.com – **practical information and resources; based in the US.**

www.walking-wounded.net – **praying for people in emotional need**

Events and conferences

Please monitor the CARE website for relevant events, especially the 'Call to Purity' events for men in Scotland, and 'The Mandate' annual men's conference in Belfast, both focussing on wholeness and accountability in men's lives.

12-step programmes

www.sauk.org – **Sexaholics Anonymous, UK and Ireland, meetings via website, plus on-line resources. Helpline 07000 725463**

www.sexaa.org – **Sex Addicts Anonymous – various meetings in England and Scotland**

www.saa-women.org – **Sex Addicts Anonymous for women**

Notes

Notes